The Sharp Minds' Cookbook

50 Vitamin and Nutrient-Packed Recipes to Maintain a Sharp Mind

BY - Zoe Moore

Copyright 2022 by Zoe Moore

Copyright Notes

I've spent a lifetime in the kitchen, and all the knowledge I've accumulated from that hasn't come without its fair share of burns and disasters. Fortunately, I'm a lot wiser from it all and am now in a place where I can share my knowledge and skills with you. However, that doesn't mean anyone can use my content for any purpose they please. This book has been copyrighted as a way to protect my story, knowledge, and recipes, so I can continue sharing them with others into the future.

Do not make any print or electronic reproductions, sell, re-publish, or distribute this book in parts or as a whole unless you have express written consent from me or my team.

This is a condensed version of the copyright license, but it's everything you need to know in a nutshell. Please help protect my life's work and all the burns and melted spatulas I have accumulated in order to publish this book.

Table of Contents

Introduction 6

   (1) Tempting Thai Curry... 8

   (2) Roasted Red Pepper and Potatoes... 11

   (3) Yummy Meat and Mushroom Casserole 14

   (4) Superb Halibut and Spinach Duo 17

   (5) Sweet Potato and Garbanzo Beans 20

   (6) Potatoes with a Creamy Filling 23

   (7) Party Time Lasagna... 26

   (8) Cheesy Zucchini 30

   (9) Spaghetti with Soya Chunks 33

   (10) Simple Fried Rice.. 36

   (11) White Fish with Coconut Milk 39

   (12) Chicken with Mushroom Sauce 42

   (13) Mouth-Watering Meatballs 45

   (14) Tofu Curry 48

   (15) Halibut with Green Sauce... 51

   (16) Ratatouille... 53

   (17) Broccoli Pasta... 55

   (18) Vegan Balls.. 58

   (19) Crunchy Pea Patties.. 61

(20) Vegetable Soup 64

(21) Baked Vegetable Fritters 67

(22) Tomato Soup 70

(23) Lettuce Wraps 73

(24) Mushroom Caps 76

(25) Delicious Grilled Chicken 79

(26) Beans and Cauliflower 82

(27) Tilapia with Nuts and Olives 85

(28) Mushrooms and Beans 88

(29) Sausage and Shrimp Combo 91

(30) Healthy Green Beans 94

(31) Peppy Tuna and Avocado Salad 97

(32) Chargrilled Bell Pepper and Cajun Fish 100

(33) Creamy Salsa Fish 103

(34) Tasty Chicken Wings 106

(35) Utterly Delicious All in One 109

(36) Chef's Choice Casserole 112

(37) Spicy Paneer 115

(38) Spicy Veggies and Shrimp 118

(39) Sweet Potatoes with Ginger 121

(40) Salmon with Coconut and Cabbage 123

(41) Cabbage with Peas 126

(42) Cod with Tomatoes 129

(43) Baked Carrots, Beetroot, and Peas 132

(44) Cauliflower Rice 135

(45) Multi-Layer Burgers 138

(46) Honey Mustard Fillets 141

(47) Garlic Flavored Soya Chunk Skewers 144

(48) Novel Pizza Crust 147

(49) Butternut Squash with Lemon Ginger Sauce 151

(50) Delicious Tacos 153

About the Author 156

Author's Afterthoughts 157

Introduction

Maintaining a sharp mind becomes increasingly difficult as you get older, so don't wait until you're 80 to start making those lifestyle changes. There's no better time to start than today, so we hope you're excited about this cooking journey we're beginning! Before we get started, though, you need to let go of the misconception that eating healthy means you'll be eating salads and raw veggies from now on. While you can do that, we've gone above and beyond to make sure these recipes are actually delicious and REAL. With that said, let's get started!

Over the next couple of days, we'll be making dishes like burgers, tacos, lasagna, and even fried rice. You heard right! All of that and much more. Yes, you are flipping through the correct cookbook. We didn't want our meals to be bland, and we wanted them to be things you actually crave. That's why we went out of our way to make the necessary healthy substitutions so that they're packed with vitamins and nutrients!

The Sharp Minds' Cookbook will make being on your A-game extremely easy, and we're excited for you to start experiencing the many benefits of healthy home-cooked meals. Your memory and energy levels will improve massively for starters, so make sure to go in for seconds and even third servings! However, consistency is key. Pick up the chopping board and start cooking. Today is day one of improved mental agility. Let's go!

xxxxxxxxxxxxxxxxxxxxxxxxxxxxxxxxxxxxxxxxxxxxxxx

(1) Tempting Thai Curry

It is a typical Thai recipe that uses coconut cream and curry paste. It is easy to prepare the curry paste at home. But if you want to save time, you can buy ready-made paste from the market. The taste will be equally good. Fish and broccoli are very healthy on their own. But olives and soy protein powder enhance the nutritional value of the recipe.

Total Prep Time: 30 minutes

Yield: 4

List of Ingredients:

- 1 oz avocado oil
- 1 lb. white fish fillets (cut into pieces)
- 2 cups broccoli (cut into small florets)
- 1 oz butter
- 1 oz peanut butter
- 16 oz coconut cream
- 4 oz cilantro (chopped)
- 2 oz olives
- 1 tablespoon soy protein powder
- 1 pinch cayenne pepper
- 1/4 teaspoons black pepper
- 1/4 teaspoons salt

Curry paste:

- 5 sprigs curry leaves
- 1/4 teaspoons coriander powder
- 1/8 teaspoons turmeric powder
- 1/8 teaspoons cumin powder
- 2 tablespoons water

xxxxxxxxxxxxxxxxxxxxxxxxxxxxxxxxxxxxxxxxxxx

How to Cook:

Grease a baking tray with avocado oil. Place the fillets on it and spread plain butter, black pepper, and salt on them.

Prepare the curry paste by grinding the curry leaves with spices. Add water.

Mix the paste with cilantro, coconut cream, soy protein, and olives. Pour this mixture on the fillets.

Place the baking tray in a preheated oven at a temperature of 400°F for about 20 minutes.

In the meantime, boil the broccoli in salted water. Remove the water and sprinkle cayenne pepper on it. Garnish with peanut butter.

Serve the fillets and broccoli together.

(2) Roasted Red Pepper and Potatoes

Surprise your family with this peppy dish. Everyone loves potatoes, and when you add some bell peppers, they become irresistible. The best part is that you only need 5 ingredients to prepare this recipe. It offers good health on your platter without the need for any elaborate preparation.

Total Prep Time: 25 minutes

Yield: 4

List of Ingredients:

- 4 bell peppers (red)
- 4 potatoes
- 2 tablespoons butter
- 2 tablespoons olive oil (extra virgin)
- ¼ teaspoons salt

xxxxxxxxxxxxxxxxxxxxxxxxxxxxxxxxxxxxxxxxxxxxx

How to Cook:

Heat the oven beforehand to a temperature of 450°F.

Wash the bell peppers and cut them in half lengthwise.

Use one paring knife to cut the stems. Scoop out the membranes and seeds.

Grease one baking sheet with some butter. Place the bell peppers on it with the cut side facing down. Arrange them on one half of the sheet.

Peel and cut the potatoes into small pieces. Place them on the other half of the sheet.

Drizzle olive oil on top. Roast them for about 25 minutes until the peppers' skins become fully wrinkled. You can rotate the sheet to cook them evenly.

Allow the contents to cool down for 1-2 minutes. Then transfer the peppers and potatoes to two separate bowls and cover them.

Let them cool for 30 minutes.

When the peppers are cool, remove their skins.

Take a large bowl and mix the potatoes and the peppers. Add the salt and toss to spread it evenly.

(3) Yummy Meat and Mushroom Casserole

Your family will enjoy this sumptuous treat. It contains the goodness of meat, mushrooms, and eggs. Moreover, it has heavy cream and mozzarella cheese that enrich it. Tomato sauce will enhance the flavor and make the dish more appealing. Even though you will have to spend a little more time cooking it, you will win appreciation for your efforts.

Total Prep Time: 50 minutes

Yield: 4

List of Ingredients:

- 8 oz meat (processed and ground)
- 8 oz mushrooms
- 8 oz mozzarella cheese cubes
- 4 eggs
- 4 oz heavy cream
- 2 oz olive oil
- 2 oz tomato sauce
- 1 green bell pepper
- 1 red bell pepper
- 1 onion
- 1 garlic clove
- 1/2 teaspoons oregano
- 1/2 teaspoons rosemary
- 1/2 teaspoons basil
- 1/2 teaspoons salt
- 1/4 teaspoons chili powder (optional)

xxxxxxxxxxxxxxxxxxxxxxxxxxxxxxxxxxxxxxxxxxxxxx

How to Cook:

Heat half of the oil in a pan and cook the meat and mushroom until they become slightly brown.

Whip the eggs, heavy cream, tomato sauce, salt, and chili powder in a bowl.

Mince the garlic clove, cut the onion into small pieces, wash and cut the peppers.

Grease a baking dish. Put the meat, mushrooms, mozzarella cheese cubes, and peppers in it. Pour the whipped egg mixture on them.

Spread the garlic and onion on top. Then sprinkle oregano, rosemary, and basil.

Place the dish in the oven and bake for 45 minutes at a temperature of 350°F. Allow it to cool for a few minutes, then serve.

(4) Superb Halibut and Spinach Duo

Here is a recipe that has double benefits. You can enjoy the goodness of fish as well as spinach. Moreover, when you add sour cream, cheese, and butter, you give an exotic taste to the dish. You can use any cooking oil for this dish. But avocado oil is an excellent choice to meet the nutritional needs of your family.

Total Prep Time: 20 minutes

Yield: 4

List of Ingredients:

- 1 lb. halibut fillets
- 4 cups spinach (chopped)
- 8 oz sour cream
- 5 tablespoons cheese (grated)
- 2 tablespoons butter
- 1 teaspoon avocado oil
- 1 teaspoon flax seeds
- 1 sprig parsley (chopped)
- 1 sprig celery (chopped)
- 1 onion (chopped finely)
- 1 oz tomato puree
- 1 oz acai berries
- 1/4 teaspoons black pepper
- 1/4 teaspoons salt

xxxxxxxxxxxxxxxxxxxxxxxxxxxxxxxxxxxxxxxxxxxxx

How to Cook:

Heat the oven in advance to a temperature of 400°F. Use a brush to apply butter on a baking tray.

Season the fillets with some pepper and salt. Put them on the baking tray.

Take a bowl and mix sour cream, cheese, acai berries, flax seeds, parsley, and celery.

Spread the cream mixture on the fillets.

Bake for 20 minutes.

In the meantime, heat the oil in a pan. Put the onions in it. Sauté them until they become translucent. Add the tomato puree and cook for 2 minutes. Then put the chopped spinach leaves in it. Cook for another 5 minutes. Sprinkle the remaining pepper and salt.

Take out the fish fillets from the oven and arrange them on a platter. Spread the cooked spinach on it evenly and serve.

(5) Sweet Potato and Garbanzo Beans

Sweet potatoes have lots of fiber, minerals, and vitamins. They are conducive to gut health. Besides this, they also support brain function, vision, and the immune system. Garbanzo beans can help in controlling your appetite and managing your weight. They have plenty of protein and help keep blood sugar in check. So, this recipe is a sure shot means to boost your health.

Total Prep Time: 30 minutes

Yield: 6

List of Ingredients:

- 15 oz garbanzo beans (canned, drained, rinsed)
- 8 oz spinach (chopped)
- 2 sweet potatoes (cut into cubes)
- 2 oz olive oil
- 1 oz butter
- 1 tablespoon peanut butter
- 1 clove garlic (minced)
- 1" piece ginger (minced)
- 1 spring onion (cut finely)
- 14 oz tomato puree
- 14 oz soy milk
- 1 cinnamon
- 1 cardamom
- 1 clove
- 1/4 teaspoons turmeric
- 1/2 teaspoons cumin powder
- 1/4 teaspoons chili powder
- 1/4 teaspoons black pepper
- 1/2 teaspoons salt
- 2 oz olives (sliced)
- 1 bunch cilantro (chopped finely)

xxxxxxxxxxxxxxxxxxxxxxxxxxxxxxxxxxxxxxxxxxxxx

How to Cook:

Heat the oil and add cinnamon, cardamom, and clove.

Sauté garlic, ginger, and onion for 5 minutes.

Then add turmeric and cook for a minute.

Put the garbanzo beans, sweet potatoes, spinach, tomato puree, and soy milk in the pan.

Add butter, chili powder, black pepper, salt, and cumin powder.

Cook for 5 minutes on medium heat.

When the contents start boiling, reduce the heat and simmer for 15 minutes.

Garnish with olives, cilantro, spring onion, and peanut butter.

(6) Potatoes with a Creamy Filling

You will have to preheat the oven and bake the potatoes. In the meantime, you can prepare the filling. It is better to whisk the sour cream and lemon juice separately and add it to the bean mixture. Do not mash the beans too much. Be careful while filling the potatoes so that they do not split apart. You can make the dish look attractive by pouring the remaining sour cream mixture on top and garnishing it with cilantro and parsley.

Total Prep Time: 35 minutes

Yield: 4

List of Ingredients:

- 4 large potatoes
- 4 oz sour cream
- 8 oz black beans (canned, drained, rinsed)
- 1 teaspoon lemon juice
- 1 onion
- 1 garlic clove
- 1/2 teaspoons salt
- 1/2 teaspoons pepper
- 2 oz olive oil
- 2 oz cilantro (chopped finely)
- 1 sprig parsley (chopped finely)

xxxxxxxxxxxxxxxxxxxxxxxxxxxxxxxxxxxxxxxxxxxx

How to Cook:

Heat the oven to a temperature of 350°F. Grease a baking tray.

Place the potatoes on it. Bake for 30 minutes.

In the meantime, whisk the sour cream and lemon juice in a bowl.

Take a pan and heat olive oil. Mince the garlic and cut the onion finely. Sauté them in the oil.

Then put the beans in the pan. Add salt and pepper.

Cook for 5 minutes. Stir frequently. After that, remove the pan from heat and mash the beans.

When the baked potatoes are cool, scoop out their inner portion.

Add the inner portion of the potatoes to the mashed beans. Mix half of the sour cream mixture with the beans.

Fill the potatoes with this bean mixture. If some bean mixture remains, place it around the potatoes.

Pour the remaining half of the sour cream mixture on the potatoes.

Sprinkle cilantro and parsley on it before serving.

(7) Party Time Lasagna

Here is an elaborate recipe that requires some time and patience. But it is very healthy and tasty. Instead of using the regular variety of lasagna, you will be using zucchini noodles. So, first, you will have to use a cabbage shredder or vegetable peeler to make thin slices of zucchini. Then, you can prepare the sauce. Finally, arrange the layers of lasagna and bake for 30 minutes at a temperature of 400°F. Place it in the fridge to solidify it. You can serve it cold or heat it before serving.

Total Prep Time: 1 hour

Yield: 6

List of Ingredients:

- 2 cups cream cheese
- 1 cup mozzarella cheese (grated)
- 1 cup spinach (chopped and boiled)
- 3 eggs (hard-boiled)
- 4 oz olives
- 5 thick and straight zucchini

Sauce:

- 1 onion
- 1 cup mushrooms
- 1 cup soy granules
- 2 cloves garlic
- 1 tablespoon avocado oil
- 1 sprig parsley
- 1 sprig basil
- 1 sprig oregano
- 1 sprig thyme
- 1 bay leaf
- 1 pinch cayenne pepper
- 1/4 teaspoons black pepper
- 1/2 teaspoons garlic powder
- 1/2 teaspoons salt
- 2 cups tomato puree
- 8 oz water
- 10 oz zucchini cores (left after making sheets of lasagna)

xx

How to Cook:

Make zucchini noodles:

Take a cabbage shredder or vegetable peeler and cut out thin slices.

Make the sauce:

Chop the onion, mushrooms, garlic, parsley, basil, oregano, thyme, and cores of the zucchini. Soak the soy granules in warm water.

Put 1-tablespoon of avocado oil in a stockpot and sauté garlic and onions in it.

Drain the water from the soy granules and put them in the pot. Allow them to become slightly brown.

Then, add chopped zucchini and mushrooms. Cook until they become tender.

Add tomato puree, all the herbs and spices, and water. Stir well.

Cook on low heat for about 20 minutes. Stir frequently so that the sauce does not stick to the pot.

Remove it from the heat source after it becomes sufficiently thick and allow it to cool.

Make lasagna:

Preheat oven to 400°F. Chop the olives and boiled eggs.

Cut zucchini noodles according to the size of the baking sheet you will use.

Put some sauce at the bottom of the baking sheet and place zucchini noodles on it.

Cover the noodles with a quarter cup of cream cheese, mozzarella cheese, spinach, boiled eggs, olives, and the prepared sauce. Then put a layer of zucchini noodles on it.

Repeat the layers several times until all the ingredients are on the baking sheet.

Bake it for about 30 minutes. Allow it to cool.

Then put it into the fridge so that it can solidify a bit.

You can serve it cold or heat it before serving.

(8) Cheesy Zucchini

It is a paleo-friendly, gluten-free, and low-carb recipe. Although, only a few ingredients are needed to prepare it. But the result is enrapturing. You have to cut open the zucchinis and fill them with the meat mixture. You can use any variety of meat and hot and sweet sauce according to your preference. All of them contribute to making a luscious dish.

Total Prep Time: 45 minutes

Yield: 4

List of Ingredients:

- 4 medium-sized zucchinis
- 1 lb. meat (processed and ground)
- 1 onion
- 1 oz butter
- 4 oz hot and sweet sauce
- 2 oz mozzarella cheese
- 2 oz cream cheese
- 1/4 teaspoons salt
- 1/4 teaspoons pepper

xxxxxxxxxxxxxxxxxxxxxxxxxxxxxxxxxxxxxxxxxxxxx

How to Cook:

Put the butter in a pan and melt it.

Cut the onion. Sauté it in the pan, then add the meat. Sprinkle pepper and salt on it. Cook for 10 minutes.

Add the hot and sweet sauce.

Cook for 5 minutes.

Cut a slit in each zucchini lengthwise. Scoop out the inner portion.

Put the zucchinis on a small baking tray. Fill the meat mixture in them.

Spread the cream cheese on each of them. Grate the mozzarella cheese and sprinkle it on top.

Cover the tray with foil.

Heat the oven to a temperature of 400°F. Bake for 30 minutes.

You can serve it hot or keep it aside for later use.

(9) Spaghetti with Soya Chunks

Spaghetti is cooked very frequently in almost all homes. So, you can try out this variation for your family. It is a sumptuous dish that is filling and nutritious. Parmesan and mozzarella cheeses give additional value to this dish. Moreover, the soya chunks add some crunchiness and make the food enjoyable.

Total Prep Time: 40 minutes

Yield: 4

List of Ingredients:

- 8 oz spaghetti
- 4 oz soya chunks
- 4 oz parmesan cheese
- 2 oz mozzarella cheese
- 4 tomatoes
- 2 onions
- 2 oz olive oil
- 2 oz hot and sweet sauce
- 1/2 teaspoons salt
- 1/2 teaspoons pepper

xxxxxxxxxxxxxxxxxxxxxxxxxxxxxxxxxxxxxxxxxxxxx

How to Cook:

Soak the soya chunks in hot water for half an hour before you start cooking.

Wash the tomatoes and cut them into small pieces. Chop the onions into thin slices. Grate the cheeses.

Cook the spaghetti in hot water with a little bit of salt. When it becomes tender, drain the water and keep it aside.

Take a big pan and heat the oil in it. Sauté the onion slices and tomato pieces. Then, squeeze out the water from the soya chunks and put them in the pan. Add pepper and salt. Cook for 5 minutes until they become brown and slightly crispy.

Grease a baking dish. Heat the oven to a temperature of 350°F.

Put half of the spaghetti on the baking dish. Then, spread some onion slices, tomato pieces, soya chunks, and hot and sweet sauce.

Place the rest of the spaghetti on it. Spread the remaining onion slices, tomato pieces, soya chunks, and hot and sweet sauce on it. Spread the grated cheeses on top.

Cover the baking dish with foil and place it in the oven.

Cook for 30 minutes.

Then, remove the cover and cook for 5 minutes. Allow it to rest for a few minutes before serving.

(10) Simple Fried Rice

You can use fresh rice or leftover rice for this recipe. It is a convenient and satisfying dish that you can prepare whenever you run out of ideas for dinner. It is not necessary to use only these vegetables. Feel free to use any other vegetables that you have at home. Usually, it is good to cut all the vegetables to the same size. You can cut them into thin slices to make the dish more presentable if you like.

Total Prep Time: 20 minutes

Yield: 4

List of Ingredients:

- 2 cups rice
- 4 oz peas
- 2 oz carrots
- 1 green bell pepper
- 1 red bell pepper
- 2 eggs
- 1 oz butter
- 1 oz olive oil
- 1 onion
- 1/2 teaspoons salt
- 1/4 teaspoons pepper
- 2 oz cilantro (chopped finely)

xxxxxxxxxxxxxxxxxxxxxxxxxxxxxxxxxxxxxxxxxxxxx

How to Cook:

Wash and cut the vegetables into small pieces. Whip the eggs in a small bowl.

Cook the rice as usual and keep it aside.

Boil the peas until they are soft.

Put some butter in a pan and make scrambled eggs.

Cut the onion into thin slices. Add the remaining butter to the pan and sauté the onion slices. Then add all the vegetables and stir fry them.

Take a large pot and heat olive oil in it. Put the cooked rice and vegetables into it. Break the scrambled eggs into small pieces and add them to the rice. Sprinkle pepper and salt.

Stir so that everything gets mixed properly. Cover the dish and cook for 5 minutes.

Then remove the cover and cook for a few minutes.

Remove from heat and transfer to a serving dish. Sprinkle cilantro on top and serve it hot.

(11) White Fish with Coconut Milk

Here is a quick recipe that is easy to make and good for your health. You may use any variety of white fish fillets for this recipe. It is not necessary to use coconut oil. If you prefer to use some other oil, go ahead and do it. Coconut milk contains many nutrients and will give a remarkable taste to the dish. Lemon juice will make it a bit tangy. As a result, you will have a delicious dish to impress everyone.

Total Prep Time: 15 minutes

Yield: 4

List of Ingredients:

- 4 white fish fillets
- 1 tablespoon coconut oil
- 2 oz butter
- 4 oz coconut milk
- 1 onion (chopped finely)
- 1 teaspoon lemon juice
- 1/2 teaspoons salt
- 1/4 cup cilantro (chopped finely)
- 1 sprig of fresh parsley (chopped finely)

xxxxxxxxxxxxxxxxxxxxxxxxxxxxxxxxxxxxxxxxxxxxx

How to Cook:

Apply some salt on both sides of the fillets.

Heat the oil in a pan and sauté the onion for a few seconds.

Then, add butter. After it melts completely, put the fillets in it.

Fry the fillets for 4 to 5 minutes.

Then, flip them and fry them on the other side for another 4 to 5 minutes.

Take them out of the pan and place them in a serving dish.

Lower the heat and put lemon juice in the pan. After that, pour the coconut milk into it.

Allow it to boil for about 5 minutes until it thickens. Stir occasionally.

Then, pour it on the fillets.

Garnish with cilantro and parsley before serving.

(12) Chicken with Mushroom Sauce

Here are a creamy chicken and mushroom treat for your family. It is also a means to boost their health. Both chicken and mushrooms are nutritious and filling. You can buy whole chicken breasts and cut them into cubes or purchase ready-made cubes. Similarly, you may prepare mushroom soup on your own or get canned mushroom soup from the market.

Total Prep Time: 30 minutes

Yield: 4

List of Ingredients:

- 2 chicken breasts (cut into cubes)
- 8 oz mushrooms
- 4 oz cream of mushroom soup
- 1 oz butter
- 1 oz olive oil
- 1/4 teaspoons pepper
- 1/2 teaspoons salt
- 1 sprig parsley (chopped finely)

xxxxxxxxxxxxxxxxxxxxxxxxxxxxxxxxxxxxxxxxxxxxx

How to Cook:

Place the chicken cubes in a large dish. Add some pepper and salt. Toss to coat them evenly.

Heat half of the oil and butter in a pan. Cook the cubes in it for 10 minutes. Take them out in a dish. Cover them with foil so that they remain warm.

Wipe the pan and put the remaining oil and butter. Put the mushrooms in it. Add the remaining pepper and salt.

Cook for 5 minutes.

Pour the cream of mushroom soup and cook for 5 minutes.

Then add the chicken cubes to it.

Cook for 10 minutes.

Sprinkle parsley and serve.

(13) Mouth-Watering Meatballs

You will be surprised to find that the meatballs turn out to be so tasty and tender. Your family will love its rich and creamy gravy. The best part is that you are going to use olive oil to prepare them. So, they will be super healthy! Keep in mind that the balls will taste better if you sauté garlic and onion before mixing them with the other ingredients.

Total Prep Time: 25 minutes

Yield: 4

List of Ingredients:

- 1 lb. meat (processed and ground)
- 1 egg
- 1 red onion
- 1 garlic clove
- 1 oz olive oil
- 2 oz breadcrumbs
- 1/2 teaspoons salt
- 1/2 teaspoons pepper
- 1 tablespoon oregano
- 1 tablespoon rosemary
- 2 cups broth
- 4 oz cream cheese
- 1 sprig of fresh parsley

xxxxxxxxxxxxxxxxxxxxxxxxxxxxxxxxxxxxxxxxxxxx

How to Cook:

Heat a little olive oil in a skillet. Sauté garlic and onion in it. Allow it to cool.

Whip the egg in a small bowl.

Take a big bowl and mix the meat, whipped egg, sauteed garlic and onion, breadcrumbs, oregano, rosemary, and a quarter spoon of salt and pepper.

Mix the ingredients properly. Then form 12 meatballs with the mixture.

Pour the remaining olive oil into a pot and heat it on the stovetop. Pour the broth into it. Lower the heat when the broth starts boiling.

Add the meatballs to it. Season it with the remaining salt and pepper.

Cover the pot and cook for 20 minutes.

Then take out the meatballs. Add cream cheese to the broth and stir well. Cook for 2 to 3 minutes until it thickens a bit.

Put the meatballs back into the creamy gravy and simmer for 2 minutes. Garnish with finely chopped parsley and serve it hot.

(14) Tofu Curry

You can buy a firm variety of tofu for this recipe. Usually, if you want the slices to be crispier, you should use the extra-firm variety of tofu. And medium tofu for softer tofu slices. You will have to cut it into thin slices before cooking. Cut the bell peppers into thin, long pieces. You may use frozen or fresh peas, whichever is more convenient for you. Serve plenty of gravy with each tofu slice to enjoy the rich taste of the recipe.

Total Prep Time: 20 minutes

Yield: 4

List of Ingredients:

- 12 oz tofu (firm variety)
- 8 oz coconut milk
- 2 oz olive oil
- 1 green bell pepper
- 1 red bell pepper
- 1 oz peas
- 1 onion
- 1 garlic clove
- 1 teaspoon lemon juice
- 1/2 teaspoons salt
- 1/2 teaspoons pepper

xxxxxxxxxxxxxxxxxxxxxxxxxxxxxxxxxxxxxxxxxxxxx

How to Cook:

Cut the tofu into thin slices of 2" x 3". They should be 2 mm to 3 mm thick. Wash the peppers and cut them into small pieces. Chop the garlic and onion.

If you prefer the peas to be soft, boil them separately until they become tender.

Take a pan and heat half of the oil. Place the tofu slices in it.

Cook for 3 to 4 minutes. Flip the slices when one side becomes golden brown and crispy. In the same way, cook on the other side for 3 to 4 minutes.

Remove the tofu slices from the pan and keep them in a flat dish.

Add the remaining oil to the pan and sauté garlic and onion. After 2 minutes, add the peppers and peas to it.

Then put the slices in the pan. Pour coconut milk and lemon juice.

Season with pepper and salt.

Stir gently and cook for 10 minutes until the gravy becomes slightly thick.

Transfer it to a serving dish and serve it hot.

(15) Halibut with Green Sauce

It is easy to prepare this dish. You can put the ingredients for the sauce in a food processor and blend them to prepare the green sauce. If you want to make it a bit spicy, you can add a tablespoon of some hot sauce to it. Then lightly fry the fillets in olive oil. After that, you have to pour the sauce on the cooked fillets and serve the tasty and healthy dish.

Total Prep Time: 10 minutes

Yield: 4

List of Ingredients:

- 4 halibut fillets
- 2 oz olive oil
- 1 raw mango
- 1 red onion
- 1 garlic clove
- 1 tablespoon lemon juice
- 1 bunch cilantro
- 1/2 teaspoons salt
- 1/2 teaspoons pepper

xxxxxxxxxxxxxxxxxxxxxxxxxxxxxxxxxxxxxxxxxxxxx

How to Cook:

Wash and cut the raw mango, red onion, and cilantro. Mince the garlic clove.

Put all these ingredients in your food processor. Add the lemon juice and some salt and pepper.

Blend them and make a smooth green sauce.

Apply pepper and salt on either side of the fillets.

Take a big pan and heat the oil. Then place the fillets in it. Cook for 4 minutes, then flip them. Let them cook for another 4 minutes.

Serve them on a large flat dish and pour the green sauce evenly on top.

(16) Ratatouille

It is a simple and nutritious recipe that you can make quite often. You can vary the proportion of the vegetables according to your choice. If you want to use fresh herbs, you can use them instead of dried ones. You can cook the vegetables for a lesser time if you want them to be a little firm. But if you like them to be very soft, cook them for a longer time. You can stir them frequently so that they become slightly mashed.

Total Prep Time: 20 minutes

Yield: 4

List of Ingredients:

- 4 brinjals
- 1 zucchini
- 1 capsicum
- 4 tomatoes
- 1 onion
- 1 garlic clove
- 1 oz olive oil
- 1 tablespoon basil
- 1 tablespoon oregano
- 1 tablespoon rosemary
- 1/2 teaspoons salt
- 1/4 teaspoons pepper

xxxxxxxxxxxxxxxxxxxxxxxxxxxxxxxxxxxxxxxxxxxxxx

How to Cook:

Wash and cut the vegetables. Mince the garlic and chop the onion into small pieces.

Take a pan and heat the oil in it. Sauté garlic and onion.

Add the vegetables, pepper, and salt. Stir to mix everything properly.

Cook on medium heat for 15 minutes until the vegetables become soft.

Sprinkle basil, oregano, and rosemary. Cook for another 5 minutes.

Transfer it to a serving dish and serve it while it is hot.

(17) Broccoli Pasta

You can put some salt in the water and boil the pasta. Drain it and keep it aside. In the meantime, roast the broccoli. Fry the chicken and slice it thinly. Finally, you can mix the pasta, broccoli, chicken slices, and other ingredients and serve it hot or cold. It is a healthy recipe as it contains broccoli, chicken, cheese, and avocado oil.

Total Prep Time: 1 hour

Yield: 6

List of Ingredients:

- 2 cups broccoli (cut into bite-sized florets)
- 2 cups pasta
- 2 oz avocado oil
- 1 tablespoon butter
- 2 chicken breasts (skinless, boneless)
- 1 sprig rosemary (chopped finely)
- 1 sprig thyme (chopped finely)
- 1 sprig parsley (chopped finely)
- 1 oz olives (cut into halves)
- 1 clove garlic (crushed)
- 1 tablespoon lemon juice
- 2 oz parmesan shavings
- 1/4 teaspoons black pepper
- 1/4 teaspoons salt

xxxxxxxxxxxxxxxxxxxxxxxxxxxxxxxxxxxxxxxxxxxx

How to Cook:

Heat the oven beforehand to a temperature of 400°F.

Boil salted water and cook pasta in it. Drizzle some avocado oil on it.

Grease a baking tray. Put broccoli in it. Then, drizzle some oil on it. Season according to taste. Roast for 25 minutes until it is slightly charred.

Season the chicken with pepper and salt.

Heat oil and butter in one heavy-bottomed frying pan.

Put the chicken in it. Fry it on one side until it becomes crispy and golden. Then turn it and put the lid.

Cook for five minutes on medium heat.

After that, remove the lid, raise the heat, and fry it again for a few minutes to make it crisp. Take it out of the vessel and let it rest for five minutes before slicing it thinly.

Then, take one large bowl and gently toss pasta with broccoli, sliced chicken, parmesan shavings, garlic, parsley, rosemary, thyme, olives, and lemon juice.

Season once again according to taste. You can serve it hot or cold.

(18) Vegan Balls

You can just fry the vegan balls and serve them with some sauce or dip as a side dish. Otherwise, you can use the complete recipe and add them to the gravy and use it as a main dish. According to your choice, you can use the seasoned variety of breadcrumbs or the plain ones. If you like, you can even add some more variety of vegetables like carrots or beetroot. Remember to boil them and squeeze out as much water as possible before mashing them.

Total Prep Time: 25 minutes

Yield: 4

List of Ingredients:

- 2 potatoes
- 1 cauliflower
- 1 oz peas
- 1 onion
- 8 oz breadcrumbs
- 4 oz oil (for frying)
- 2 cups vegetable stock
- 1/2 teaspoons salt
- 1/4 teaspoons pepper
- 1 sprig parsley
- 1 stalk celery

xxxxxxxxxxxxxxxxxxxxxxxxxxxxxxxxxxxxxxxxxx

How to Cook:

Peel the potatoes and cut the cauliflower into small florets.

Boil the potatoes, cauliflower florets, and peas for 10 to 15 minutes until they become tender.

Drain the vegetable stock and keep it aside.

Mash the potatoes, cauliflower, and peas coarsely.

Add the breadcrumbs.

Sprinkle pepper and half of the salt.

Mix everything well.

Then make 12 balls with the mixture.

Take a pan and heat oil in it. Then fry the balls.

Put some oil in another pan and sauté the onions. Then add the vegetable stock to it. When it starts boiling, reduce the heat and cook until it becomes slightly thick.

Add the vegetable balls and the remaining salt. Simmer for 5 minutes.

Sprinkle finely chopped parsley and celery on top. Serve it hot.

(19) Crunchy Pea Patties

It is an easy and enjoyable dish. With this recipe, you can make 8 patties out of it and fry them until they become golden brown and crispy. Place the pea patties on a serving plate. Put the blueberries and raspberries in between and around them. Place thin slices of olives on top of the pea patties. Finally, put half a teaspoon of tomato sauce on each.

Total Prep Time: 15 minutes

Yield: 8 pieces

List of Ingredients:

Patties:

- 8 oz green peas
- 4 oz buckwheat flour
- 1 teaspoon peanut butter
- 2 cloves garlic
- 2 spring onions
- 1 bunch cilantro
- 2 sprigs parsley
- 2 stalks celery
- 1/4 teaspoons thyme
- 1/4 teaspoons rosemary
- 1/4 teaspoons basil
- 1/4 teaspoons cumin powder
- 1/4 teaspoons black pepper
- 1/4 teaspoons salt
- 1/4 teaspoons soy protein powder
- 1/4 teaspoons baking powder
- 1 tablespoon lemon juice
- 1/2 teaspoons sesame seeds
- 1/2 tablespoons chia seeds
- 1 oz cashew nuts
- 1 oz walnuts
- 1 cup sunflower oil

Garnish:

- 2 oz olives
- 1 oz raspberries
- 1 oz blueberries
- 4 teaspoons tomato sauce

xxxxxxxxxxxxxxxxxxxxxxxxxxxxxxxxxxxxxxxxxxx

How to Cook:

Boil the peas until they become tender.

Chop the spring onions, cilantro, parsley, and celery.

Mince the garlic.

Roast the cashew nuts and walnuts. Break them into small pieces.

Put all the ingredients meant for making the patties, except the seeds, nuts, and oil, in the food processor. Blend them to make a coarse mixture.

Transfer the mixture to a bowl and add sesame seeds, chia seeds, cashew nuts, and walnuts. Make 8-patties out of it.

Heat oil in a pan and fry them until they become golden brown. Take them out on a plate lined with a paper towel to drain the excess oil.

Place the pea patties on a serving plate. Put the blueberries and raspberries in between and around them. Place thin slices of olives on top of the pea patties. Finally, put half a teaspoon of tomato sauce on each pea patty.

(20) Vegetable Soup

Here is a rich soup recipe that contains butter and sour cream. Besides being attractive, it is healthy. Different vegetables make the dish colorful and appealing. It has a slightly tangy flavor because of the sour cream. You can even use parmesan cheese, cream cheese, or any other cheese to enhance its value and taste.

Total Prep Time: 30 minutes

Yield: 4

List of Ingredients:

- 2 carrots
- 1 beetroot
- 1 zucchini
- 1 oz peas
- 4 tomatoes
- 1 stalk celery, chopped, to garnish
- 1 sprig parsley, chopped, to garnish
- 1 onion
- 2 garlic cloves
- 1 oz butter
- 2 oz olive oil
- 1/4 teaspoons pepper
- 1/4 teaspoons salt
- 4 cups vegetable stock
- 2 oz sour cream

xxxxxxxxxxxxxxxxxxxxxxxxxxxxxxxxxxxxxxxxxxxxx

How to Cook:

Wash the vegetables and cut them into small pieces. Mince the garlic cloves and chop the onion finely.

Take a big soup pot and heat the oil in it. Sauté the garlic and onion. Then add the other vegetables and sauté them for 5 minutes.

Add vegetable stock, pepper, and salt. Cover the pan and simmer for 20 minutes.

Then remove the lid. Add the butter and cook for 5 minutes without covering the pan. Stir frequently and gently mash the vegetables with a spatula.

Remove it from heat and transfer it to a serving dish. Sprinkle finely chopped celery and parsley. Pour the sour cream on top before serving.

(21) Baked Vegetable Fritters

You will need a skillet, a muffin pan with 8 cups, and an oven to prepare this dish. Heat the oven beforehand to a temperature of 370°F. Cook the spring onions, sweet potatoes, tomatoes, and asparagus in a skillet. Whisk the eggs, kale, herbs, seasoning, soy protein, and almond milk in a bowl. Put the cooked vegetables along with the lettuce leaves and blueberries in the muffin pan cups. Pour the egg mixture on top of them. Bake them for 10 minutes.

Total Prep Time: 20 minutes

Yield: 8

List of Ingredients:

- 1 sweet potato
- 1 oz avocado oil
- 2 spring onions
- 4 tomatoes
- 1 bunch asparagus
- 1 bunch lettuce
- 2 oz blueberries
- 8 eggs
- 1 oz almond milk
- 1 teaspoon soy protein powder
- 1 bunch kale
- 1 bunch cilantro
- 2 sprigs parsley
- 1 sprig basil
- 1 sprig thyme
- 1 sprig rosemary
- 1 pinch chili powder
- 1/4 teaspoons black pepper
- 1/4 teaspoons salt

xxxxxxxxxxxxxxxxxxxxxxxxxxxxxxxxxxxxxxxxxxxx

How to Cook:

Heat the oven beforehand to a temperature of 375°F. Grease a muffin pan with 8 cups.

Wash and cut all the vegetables into small pieces.

Put avocado oil in a skillet and heat it.

Sauté the spring onions and sweet potatoes for 2 minutes.

Add the tomatoes and asparagus.

Sauté for 2-3 minutes. Then put a lid on the skillet and reduce the heat.

Cook for 5 minutes. Allow them to cool.

In the meantime, put the eggs, kale, herbs, seasoning, soy protein, and almond milk in a bowl whisk them together.

Put the cooked vegetables along with the lettuce leaves and blueberries in the muffin pan cups. Pour the whisked egg mixture on the vegetables.

Place the muffin pan in the oven.

Bake for 10 minutes.

Take the vegetable fritters out of the pan, let them cool for a few minutes, and then serve.

(22) Tomato Soup

Tomato soup is a dish that frequently occupies a place on dinner tables. It has a soothing effect and gives relief after a hectic day at work. Tomatoes contain plenty of vitamin C that boosts the immune system. It acts as a safeguard against illnesses. A variety of herbs are in the recipe that enhances the flavor and satisfies the taste buds. Serving it with heavy cream and bread makes it a wholesome dish.

Total Prep Time: 30 minutes

Yield: 4

List of Ingredients:

- 14 oz tomatoes
- 1 onion
- 2 garlic cloves
- 1 oz olive oil
- 4 oz heavy cream
- 1 teaspoon basil
- 1 teaspoon oregano
- 1 teaspoon rosemary
- 1 teaspoon thyme
- 1/2 teaspoons salt
- 1/2 teaspoons pepper
- 4 cups vegetable stock
- 2 oz cilantro (finely chopped)
- 4 toasted slices of bread

xxxxxxxxxxxxxxxxxxxxxxxxxxxxxxxxxxxxxxxxxxxxx

How to Cook:

Wash and cut the tomatoes into small pieces. Mince the garlic and chop the onions.

Take a big pot and heat the oil on medium heat. Sauté the onion and garlic for 2 to 3 minutes.

Add the tomatoes, basil, oregano, rosemary, thyme, pepper, and salt.

Cook for 5 minutes.

Then add the stock and cover the pan. Cook on low heat for 15 minutes until the tomatoes are well cooked.

Uncover the pan and cook for 5 minutes. Stir frequently. Then switch off the heat and blend the soup with a blender.

Transfer the contents to a large bowl and mix heavy cream in it.

Garnish with cilantro before serving. Cut each toasted slice of bread into four pieces and serve along with the soup.

(23) Lettuce Wraps

Soak soy granules in warm water for 15 minutes before you start cooking. Drain the water from the soy granules and cook them with garlic, onion, tomato puree, pepper, and salt. Transfer soy granules to a bowl and add spinach, oregano, chia seeds, ricotta cheese, and mozzarella cheese. Mix and combine everything thoroughly. Make 4 patties with the mixture. Then, wrap them in lettuce leaves. Arrange the tomato, onion, cucumber slices on them. Put sour cream on top of each wrap and sprinkle the fresh herbs.

Total Prep Time: 15 minutes

Yield: 4

List of Ingredients:

- 1 cup soy granules
- 2 oz chia seeds
- 10 oz spinach (chopped)
- 1 sprig oregano (chopped finely)
- 1 tablespoon avocado oil
- 1 oz tomato puree
- 1 onion (chopped)
- 1 clove garlic (minced)
- 1/4 teaspoons black pepper
- 1/8 teaspoons salt
- 4 oz ricotta cheese (crumbled)
- 4 oz mozzarella cheese (crumbled)

Garnish:

- 1 tomato (cut into thin slices)
- 1 onion (sliced thinly)
- 1/2 cucumber (sliced thinly)
- 1 tablespoon parsley (chopped finely)
- 1 tablespoon dill (chopped finely)
- 1 tablespoon mint (chopped finely)
- 4 oz sour cream
- 4 big lettuce leaves

xxxxxxxxxxxxxxxxxxxxxxxxxxxxxxxxxxxxxxxxxxxx

How to Cook:

Soak soy granules in warm water 15 minutes before you start cooking.

Sauté garlic and onion in avocado oil.

Add the tomato puree and cook for 2 minutes.

Drain the water from the soy granules and add them to the pan.

Season with black pepper and salt. Cook until soy granules become slightly brown.

Transfer the soy granules mixture to a bowl and add spinach, oregano, chia seeds, ricotta cheese, and mozzarella cheese.

Mix and combine everything thoroughly.

Make 4 patties with the mixture.

Cook them in a skillet for nearly 4 minutes on each side.

Let them cool for a few minutes. Then wrap them in lettuce leaves.

Arrange the tomato, onion, cucumber slices on them.

Put sour cream on top of each wrap and sprinkle the fresh herbs.

(24) Mushroom Caps

Mushrooms are tasty on their own. But in this recipe, you will fill a cheese mixture in mushroom caps to make them irresistible. Make it a point to dry the mushroom caps thoroughly before filling them as they give out a lot of water while cooking. You can use any variety of vinegar for this recipe. Most people like the taste of peanut butter. So, it has been added to make the dish more appealing. But if you are not fond of it, you can increase the amount of plain butter.

Total Prep Time: 15 minutes

Yield: 4

List of Ingredients:

- 20 portobello mushrooms
- 1 oz butter
- 1 oz peanut butter
- 1 garlic clove
- 1 tablespoon vinegar
- 2 tomatoes
- 4 oz sour cream
- 4 oz mozzarella cheese
- 1 sprig parsley
- 1 stalk celery
- 1/2 teaspoons salt

xxxxxxxxxxxxxxxxxxxxxxxxxxxxxxxxxxxxxxxxxxxxxx

How to Cook:

Remove the stems of the mushrooms. Wash them and dry them with paper towels.

Grate mozzarella cheese. Wash and cut the tomatoes into very tiny pieces. Chop parsley and celery finely. Crush the garlic clove.

Put the butter, peanut butter, and garlic in a pan and heat it until the butter melts.

Apply the melted butter to the outside portion of the mushroom caps and put them in a baking dish.

Mix grated mozzarella cheese, sour cream, tomatoes, vinegar, parsley, celery, and salt in a bowl.

Fill the mushroom caps with this cheese mixture.

Heat the oven to a temperature of 350°F.

Place it on a shelf in the middle of the oven.

Bake for 15 minutes until the cheese melts and the caps become golden brown.

Allow them to cool slightly before serving.

(25) Delicious Grilled Chicken

Here is a recipe in which you will first grill the chicken and then broil it. Prepare the sauce while you grill the chicken. It should be ready to be used while broiling the chicken. You will be using different varieties of cheeses such as mozzarella, parmesan, and cream cheese in this recipe. As a result, the dish will be rich and creamy.

Total Prep Time: 25 minutes

Yield: 4

List of Ingredients:

- 2 oz mozzarella cheese
- 2 oz parmesan cheese
- 1 oz cream cheese
- 1 lb. chicken breasts (boneless, sliced thinly)
- 2 oz olives

Sauce:

- 1/2 cup tomato puree
- 1 red onion
- 1 spring onion
- 2 cloves garlic
- 1 sprig thyme
- 1 sprig rosemary
- 1 sprig basil
- 1 sprig parsley
- 2 tablespoons cilantro leaves
- 1 pinch cayenne pepper
- 1/4 teaspoons black pepper
- 1/4 teaspoons salt

xxxxxxxxxxxxxxxxxxxxxxxxxxxxxxxxxxxxxxxxxxxxx

How to Cook:

Season the chicken with salt and black pepper.

Grill for about 15 minutes.

Put all the ingredients for the sauce in a food processor and blend them to make a smooth sauce.

Grease a baking tray and place the grilled chicken on it. Pour the sauce on it. Then put the olives, grated mozzarella, parmesan, and cream cheese.

Preheat the broiler for 5 minutes. Put the chicken beneath the broiler and broil for 10 minutes until cheese becomes slightly brown.

Allow it to cool, then serve.

(26) Beans and Cauliflower

Almost all the ingredients in this recipe are conducive to health. Firstly, tofu contains protein and amino acids, and cauliflower has plenty of fiber and antioxidants. Moreover, beans are a source of protein, vitamins, minerals, and antioxidants. If you want to help your family members moderate their blood sugar levels and manage their weight, you can prepare this fantastic recipe for them.

Total Prep Time: 1 hour

Yield: 8

List of Ingredients:

- 1 lb. tofu
- 1 lb. cauliflower rice
- 15 oz kidney beans (1 can drain and rinse)
- 2 oz olives
- 2 oz avocado oil
- 8 oz tomatoes
- 2 oz tomato puree
- 8 oz onions
- 4 garlic cloves
- 1 tablespoon cumin powder
- 1 teaspoon dried thyme
- 1 teaspoon dried oregano
- 1 teaspoon cocoa powder
- 1/4 teaspoons black pepper
- 1/4 teaspoons salt
- 1 tablespoon chili powder
- 10 oz water

xxxxxxxxxxxxxxxxxxxxxxxxxxxxxxxxxxxxxxxxxxxxxx

How to Cook:

Cut the onions and tomatoes into tiny pieces, mince the garlic, and cut olives into thin slices. Crumble the tofu. Put cauliflower florets in the food processor and pulse until the fragments of cauliflower look like rice.

Heat oil in a pot and sauté the onions until they become translucent. Add garlic, cook for a minute. Then add the tofu. Cook until it becomes slightly brown. Mash it with the back of a spoon if needed while cooking.

Put the herbs and spices.

Cook for 10 minutes. Then add tomatoes, tomato puree, cocoa powder, olives, and water.

Cook for about 30 minutes on medium heat. Add the beans and cauliflower.

Cook for another 10 minutes.

Allow it to cool down. Then put it in the fridge. Reheat it slowly on low heat before serving.

(27) Tilapia with Nuts and Olives

It is a rich and tasty recipe that contains cashew nuts, almonds, pecans, and pistachios. You can roast the nuts or use them raw. You should bake the fillets and cherry tomatoes in two separate baking sheets for 15 minutes. Bake the fillets with the nut mixture and the tomatoes with the herbs and other ingredients. Then serve the fish on a platter and spread the baked tomatoes on top.

Total Prep Time: 20 minutes

Yield: 4

List of Ingredients:

- 15 oz tilapia
- 1 oz cashew nuts
- 1 oz almonds
- 1 oz pecans
- 1 oz pistachios
- 2 oz olives (cut into halves)
- 1 cup cherry tomatoes
- 1 sprig thyme
- 1 sprig rosemary
- 1 sprig basil
- 1 sprig oregano
- 2 tablespoons dill
- 2 oz avocado oil
- 1 teaspoon flax seeds
- 1 teaspoon soy protein powder
- 1/4 teaspoons black pepper
- 1/4 teaspoons salt

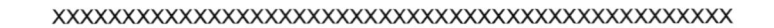

xxxxxxxxxxxxxxxxxxxxxxxxxxxxxxxxxxxxxxxxxxxxx

How to Cook:

Chop the nuts and olives finely. Keep them in a bowl and add 1-ounce avocado oil. Sprinkle some black pepper and salt. Stir the mixture.

Heat the oven beforehand to a temperature of 350°F. Put the fillets in one baking sheet and spread the nut mixture in between them and around them.

Place the cherry tomatoes in another baking sheet. Chop the herbs finely. Season the tomatoes with black pepper, salt, thyme, rosemary, basil, oregano, and dill. Add flax seeds, soy protein powder, and 1-ounce avocado oil.

Bake the fillets as well as the tomatoes for about 15 minutes. By then, the fish should become opaque.

Then serve the fish on a platter and spread the baked tomatoes on top.

(28) Mushrooms and Beans

Mushrooms are a source of selenium. They possess a lot of protein, vitamins, and antioxidants. If you want to prevent the occurrence of severe illnesses like heart disease and diabetes, make it a point to include them in your recipes. Bell peppers have a lot of vitamin C, carotenoids, and antioxidants. They are suitable for eye health and reduce the risk of various chronic diseases. So, it goes without saying that this recipe helps to guard your family members against illness.

Total Prep Time: 45 minutes

Yield: 4

List of Ingredients:

- 8 oz button mushrooms
- 8 oz kidney beans (canned, drained, rinsed)
- 8 oz black beans (canned, drained, rinsed)
- 1 bell pepper
- 8 oz tomato puree
- 1 onion
- 2 cloves garlic
- 1 green chili
- 1 teaspoon oregano
- 1/4 teaspoons cumin powder
- 1/4 teaspoons coriander powder
- 1/4 teaspoons cinnamon powder
- 1 bay leaf
- 1/4 teaspoons black pepper
- 1/4 teaspoons salt
- 1 teaspoon chili sauce
- 2 tablespoons avocado oil
- 4 oz water

Garnish:

- 1 bunch cilantro
- 2 oz sour cream
- 2 oz acai berries

xxxxxxxxxxxxxxxxxxxxxxxxxxxxxxxxxxxxxxxxxx

How to Cook:

Cut the mushrooms, bell pepper, onion, and green chili into small pieces. Mince the garlic. Chop cilantro finely.

Heat oil in a pan and sauté garlic and onion for 5 minutes. Add the green chili, oregano, cumin powder, coriander powder, and cinnamon powder.

Cook for 2 minutes.

Then, add the mushrooms and bell pepper. Stir to mix everything.

Cook for 5 minutes.

Add tomato puree and four ounces of water. Simmer for 2 minutes. Then add the bay leaf, black pepper, salt, and chili sauce. Simmer for about 2 minutes.

Put black beans and kidney beans. Cook on low heat for about 30 minutes. Stir occasionally.

Garnish with cilantro leaves, sour cream, and acai berries.

(29) Sausage and Shrimp Combo

Although the ingredients needed for this recipe are long, it is easy to prepare them. You have to cut the sausages, shrimp, and vegetables into small pieces. Season and cook the shrimp for 5 minutes. Then cook the vegetables and sausage for a few minutes. Add the shrimp and cook everything together. Finally, add the vegetable stock and cook for 5 minutes. Season according to taste. Garnish with avocado pieces, acai berries, and parsley.

Total Prep Time: 20 minutes

Yield: 4

List of Ingredients:

- 4 oz smoked sausage
- 1 lb. shrimp
- 4 bell peppers (2 green and 2 red)
- 1 zucchini
- 1 onion (sliced thinly)
- 2 cloves garlic (minced)
- 1 oz avocado oil
- 1 oz butter
- 4 oz vegetable stock
- 1 pinch chili powder
- 1/4 teaspoons coriander powder
- 1/4 teaspoons cumin powder
- 1/4 teaspoons black pepper
- 1/4 teaspoons salt
- 1 teaspoon lemon juice
- 2 oz acai berries
- 1 avocado (peeled and cut into small pieces)
- 2 sprigs parsley

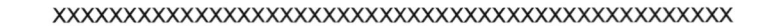

xxxxxxxxxxxxxxxxxxxxxxxxxxxxxxxxxxxxxxxxxxxxx

How to Cook:

Cut the sausages, shrimp, and vegetables into small pieces. Season the shrimp with black pepper and salt.

Heat avocado oil in a skillet on medium heat and cook the shrimp in it for 5 minutes until it becomes opaque. Take it out from the skillet and keep it aside.

Put butter in the skillet and sauté garlic and onion.

Add chili coriander powder, powder, and cumin powder.

Then put the vegetables in it and cook for 2 minutes.

Put the sausage and cook for 2 minutes.

Finally, put the cooked shrimp. Cook the entire dish for a few more minutes.

Add vegetable stock. Stir well.

Cook for 5 minutes. Sprinkle some black pepper, salt, and lemon juice.

Transfer to a serving dish.

Arrange the avocado pieces and acai berries on top.

Spread finely chopped parsley on them.

(30) Healthy Green Beans

Here is a simple yet healthy recipe that you can prepare in 15 minutes. You can use any other variety of olives according to your preference. Herbs like oregano and rosemary give added flavor to the dish. Nuts are a great source of protein. So, by including them in your recipe, you can increase the nutritional value of the beans dish.

Cooking Time required: 15 minutes

Yield: 4

List of Ingredients:

- 1 oz black olives
- 3 oz green beans
- 1 tablespoon olive oil
- 1 tomato
- 1 tablespoon capers
- 1 clove garlic
- 1 teaspoon dried oregano
- 1 teaspoon dried rosemary
- 1 sprig of fresh parsley (chopped finely)
- 1 teaspoon butter
- 1/2 oz almonds (roasted and crushed)
- 1/2 oz peanuts (roasted and crushed)
- 1 pinch cayenne pepper
- 1 pinch salt
- 2 oz vegetable broth

xxxxxxxxxxxxxxxxxxxxxxxxxxxxxxxxxxxxxxxxxxxxx

How to Cook:

String the beans and cut them into halves. Boil them for 5 minutes. When they become tender, drain the water.

Heat olive oil in another pan on medium heat.

Cut the tomato, olives, and capers.

Mince the clove of garlic.

Put them in the pan. Cook until they become tender. Pour the vegetable broth and cook on low heat for a few minutes until the liquid evaporates fully.

Put the beans, butter, oregano, rosemary, cayenne pepper, and salt.

Stir with a spatula.

Sauté them for a few minutes.

Garnish with crushed almonds, crushed peanuts, and finely chopped parsley leaves.

(31) Peppy Tuna and Avocado Salad

Fresh and uncooked vegetables are far healthier than cooked ones. Many of their nutrients get lost in the process of cooking. So, if you want to enjoy the maximum benefit of a food item, it is best to eat it in its natural form.

This salad fulfills this condition. Firstly, it provides valuable nutrients from fish and raw vegetables. Secondly, walnuts contain polyunsaturated fats, omega-3 fatty acids, and protein. They help in reducing cholesterol. Lemon juice and vinegar make it appealing to the taste buds.

Total Prep Time: 10 minutes

Yield: 4

List of Ingredients:

- 18 oz white tuna (canned in water, drained)
- 1 avocado
- 1 teaspoon vinegar
- 1 teaspoon lime juice
- 1 tomato
- 1 red onion
- 1/2 cucumber
- 1 radish
- 2 oz walnuts
- 1 oz lettuce
- 1 bell pepper
- 1 oz chives
- 1 tablespoon dill
- 1/4 teaspoons black pepper
- 1/4 teaspoons salt

xxxxxxxxxxxxxxxxxxxxxxxxxxxxxxxxxxxxxxxxxxxxxxx

How to Cook:

Open a can of white tuna and arrange them on a platter.

Cut the tomato, red onion, cucumber, radish, bell pepper into tiny pieces and put them on the fish.

Spread finely chopped dill and chives, small cut pieces of walnuts, and lettuce leaves on top.

Pour the lime juice and vinegar on them.

Season with pepper and salt.

Peel and cut the avocado into bite-size pieces and spread them on top before serving.

(32) Chargrilled Bell Pepper and Cajun Fish

You will need to heat the chargrill beforehand to prepare this recipe. If you are an adept cook and like to prepare the seasonings at home, go ahead and make the Cajun mixture on your own. Homemade stuff is always better! Otherwise, you can buy a packet of Cajun spice mixture from your grocery store. Another significant ingredient that you are going to use is avocado. It is rich in nutrients and boosts the health value of this recipe.

Total Prep Time: 20 minutes

Yield: 4

List of Ingredients:

- 4 (8 oz each) fillets (white fish)
- 1 red bell pepper
- 2 tablespoons Cajun spice mixture
- 1 avocado
- 2 shallots
- 1 tablespoon olive oil
- 1 tablespoon dill
- 1 tablespoon butter
- 1 sprig of fresh parsley
- 1/2 oz walnuts (crushed)
- 1 oz lettuce leaves
- 1 tablespoon lemon juice
- Serve with lemon wedges

xxxxxxxxxxxxxxxxxxxxxxxxxxxxxxxxxxxxxxxxxxxxxx

How to Cook:

Heat a chargrill beforehand. Deseed the bell pepper and cut it into four pieces. Spray some olive oil on both sides. Cook them on the grill for about 5 minutes on either side until they become tender. Leave them for 10 to 15 minutes and allow them to cool. Then cut them into small pieces (about 1 cm each).

Put the Cajun seasoning in a big dish and coat the fish with it. Spray some olive oil on the fish. Place baking paper (non-stick) on the chargrill. Cook the fish on it for 5 minutes on each side. Finally, check if the fish is ready and flakes easily.

Peel and cut the avocado into small pieces (1 cm).

Trim the ends of the shallot. Cut it into thin slices.

Chop the dill and parsley.

Take a bowl and mix bell pepper, avocado, dill, parsley, shallot, melted butter, and lemon juice. Sprinkle pepper and salt.

Place the fish on a serving plate and put the bell pepper mixture on it. Decorate the dish with lettuce leaves and lemon wedges before serving.

(33) Creamy Salsa Fish

You can set the oven to a temperature of 400°F and switch it on. In the meantime, you can wash and cut the tomatoes, mince the clove of garlic, and chop the onion and cilantro. Prepare the salsa. Then arrange the fillets on a baking tray, spread the salsa, cheese, and tortilla chips on them. Bake them for 15 minutes. To make the dish appealing and more nutritious, garnish with sour cream and avocado.

Total Prep Time: 15 minutes

Yield: 6

List of Ingredients:

- 24 oz cod fillets (white fish fillets)
- 4 oz cheddar cheese
- 2 oz tortilla chips
- 1 avocado
- 2 oz sour cream

Salsa:

- 2 large tomatoes
- 1 onion
- 2 oz fresh cilantro
- 1 clove of garlic
- 1/2 oz lemon juice
- 1/8 teaspoons salt
- 1/8 teaspoons black pepper

xxxxxxxxxxxxxxxxxxxxxxxxxxxxxxxxxxxxxxxxxxx

How to Cook:

Heat the oven beforehand to a temperature of 400°F. Spray some cooking oil on a baking tray.

Cut the tomatoes, onion, cilantro, and mince the clove of garlic. Put them in a big bowl and add lemon juice, salt, and black pepper. Mix them to prepare the salsa.

Place the fillets in the tray and spread the salsa on them. Grate the cheese and sprinkle it evenly. Finally, crush the tortilla chips and put them on top.

Put the baking tray in the oven without covering it. Bake the fillets for about 15 minutes. By then, the fish should be fully cooked and flake easily.

Peel the avocado and cut it into slices. Garnish the dish with slices of avocado and sour cream before serving.

(34) Tasty Chicken Wings

Do not get put off when you see the time you need to prepare it. A little patience can yield great results. Your efforts will surely be fruitful. You will be able to present a healthy dish to your family. It is better to buy the organic variety of chicken wings to get the maximum nutritional benefits.

Total Prep Time: 1 hour 30 minutes

Yield: 4

List of Ingredients:

- 1 pound chicken wings (organic)
- 1/2 teaspoons garlic salt
- 1 oz avocado oil
- 2 tablespoons butter
- 1 sprig of fresh parsley (chopped finely)
- 1 sprig cilantro (chopped finely)
- 1 pinch cayenne pepper
- 1/4 teaspoons black pepper
- 1 oz cashews (roasted and crushed)
- 1 oz peanuts (roasted and crushed)
- 2 oz blackberries (deseeded and crushed)

xxxxxxxxxxxxxxxxxxxxxxxxxxxxxxxxxxxxxxxxxxxx

How to Cook:

Heat the oven beforehand to a temperature of 250°F. Take some avocado oil and grease one baking sheet.

Put the chicken wings on this sheet. Sprinkle garlic salt on them. If you season them nicely on one side, it is sufficient.

Bake them for 45 minutes at 250°F.

Then raise the heat to a temperature of 425°F. Bake for 45 more minutes. The wings should become golden brown and shrink.

Take them out of the oven.

Leave them for five minutes.

In the meantime, mix butter, cayenne pepper, black pepper, blackberries, crushed cashews, and peanuts in a saucepan on low heat to make a sauce.

Transfer the sauce to a big bowl. Place the wings in the sauce and toss to get coated with sauce.

Garnish with parsley and cilantro before serving.

(35) Utterly Delicious All in One

Here is a superb combination of vegetarian and non-vegetarian ingredients. This recipe includes sausages, chicken, potatoes, and capsicums. You will need the oven to make this dish. Although it takes a long time to prepare, it is worth the effort. In the end, all the items will be nicely caramelized and appealing. While arranging the capsicums, potatoes, and sausage pieces around the chicken, place the veggies on top to make the dish look colorful.

Total Prep Time: 1 hour

Yield: 4

List of Ingredients:

- 2 chicken breasts
- 2 sausages
- 4 potatoes
- 1 green capsicum
- 1 yellow capsicum
- 1 red capsicum
- 1/2 teaspoons rosemary
- 2 onions
- 2 oz avocado oil
- 1/2 teaspoons oregano
- 1/2 teaspoons basil
- 1/2 teaspoons thyme
- 1/2 teaspoons parsley
- 1/2 teaspoons salt
- 1/2 teaspoons pepper

xxxxxxxxxxxxxxxxxxxxxxxxxxxxxxxxxxxxxxxxxxxxx

How to Cook:

Wash the vegetables. Cut the onion, capsicums, and potatoes into small pieces.

Take a large pan and heat half of the oil.

Cook the sausages for 2 to 3 minutes on either side until they become brown.

When they become sufficiently cool, chop them into small pieces.

Put the potatoes, capsicums, sausage pieces, and chicken in a bowl.

Add oregano, basil, rosemary, thyme, parsley, salt, pepper, and the remaining oil.

Toss to mix everything properly.

Transfer the ingredients to a roasting pan.

Keep the chicken breasts a little away from each other.

Surround them with vegetables and sausages.

Heat the oven to a temperature of 450°F.

Place the pan in the oven and cook for 50 minutes.

Insert a thermometer into the chicken and check. If it shows 165°F, it means that the chicken is ready.

Remove from the oven and serve.

(36) Chef's Choice Casserole

If you or your family members are fond of fish, cauliflower, or mushrooms, this dish is an excellent choice. It caters to a variety of tastes and is remarkably healthy. You will be using soy flakes in this recipe with high protein content. Remember to soak them in water before using them in the recipe.

Total Prep Time: 45 minutes

Yield: 6

List of Ingredients:

- 1 lb. cod fillets
- 1 lb. cauliflower (cut into small florets)
- 2 cups mushrooms (cut into wedges)
- 2 oz avocado oil
- 2 oz butter
- 2 oz peanut butter
- 1 oz soy flakes
- 1 cup cheese (grated)
- 16 oz heavy whipped cream
- 1 oz acai berries
- 1 sprig parsley (chopped finely)
- 1/4 teaspoons salt
- 1/4 teaspoons black pepper
- 2 tablespoons mustard

xxxxxxxxxxxxxxxxxxxxxxxxxxxxxxxxxxxxxxxxxxxxx

How to Cook:

Take a bowl and soak soy flakes in water. Fry the mushrooms in plain butter for 5 minutes until they become tender.

Add pepper, salt, parsley, mustard, and heavy cream. Take the soy flakes out of the water and add them to the same mixture. Reduce the heat and allow it to simmer for 10 minutes.

In the meantime, sprinkle pepper and salt on the fillets. Apply some avocado oil on a baking tray and place the fish in it. Spread half a cup of grated cheese and the entire mushroom mixture on it.

Place the baking tray in a preheated oven and bake for 30 minutes at a temperature of 350°F.

Meanwhile, boil the cauliflower and strain the water. Add peanut butter and acai berries. Mash the cauliflower coarsely and sprinkle the remaining grated cheese on top. Add salt if needed.

Serve the fillets on a platter and arrange the mashed cauliflower around them.

(37) Spicy Paneer

Paneer is a popular food item. People love it because it is tasty and easy to cook. Paneer can even be eaten raw. So, you do not have to worry about not cooking it adequately. Paneer goes well with almost every vegetable and spice. You can use olive oil or ghee to make this recipe. Stir paneer gently because it can break very easily.

Total Prep Time: 30 minutes

Yield: 4

List of Ingredients:

- 1 lb. paneer
- 4 oz peas
- 2 tomatoes
- 2 onions
- 1 teaspoon ginger and garlic paste
- 1 tablespoon tomato paste
- 1/4 teaspoons turmeric powder
- 1/4 teaspoons coriander powder
- 1/4 teaspoons chili powder
- 1/2 teaspoons salt
- 1 stick cinnamon
- 2 cardamoms
- 2 cloves
- 2 oz olive oil
- 1 oz heavy cream
- 2 cups water
- 2 oz cilantro (chopped finely)
- 1 oz cashew nuts (roasted and cut into pieces)

xxxxxxxxxxxxxxxxxxxxxxxxxxxxxxxxxxxxxxxxxxxx

How to Cook:

Wash the tomatoes.

Cut the tomatoes and onions into small pieces.

Cut the paneer into small cubes.

Boil the peas for 10 minutes so that they become soft. Drain the water and keep them aside.

Take a large pan and heat oil.

Sauté the onions and tomatoes for 2 to 3 minutes. Add ginger and garlic paste, tomato paste, turmeric, coriander powder, chili powder, salt, cardamoms, cloves, and cinnamon.

Stir to mix everything properly.

Cook for 2 minutes.

Add paneer and boiled peas. Pour 2 cups of water. Stir well to combine. Cover the pan and cook for 15 minutes.

Then remove the lid and add the heavy cream.

Cook without covering for 10 minutes.

Transfer to a serving dish. Garnish with cilantro and cashew nuts before serving.

(38) Spicy Veggies and Shrimp

You need to spend some time preparing the items for cooking. Peel the shrimp. Wash the vegetables thoroughly before cutting them into small pieces. Arrange them in layers in the baking dish. Then lay the shrimp on top. Prepare a smooth mixture with the other ingredients and spread it evenly on the shrimp. After 40 minutes of baking, you will be able to present a rich and creamy treat to your family. It may be a bit spicy, too.

Total Prep Time: 40 minutes

Yield: 8

List of Ingredients:

- 8 shrimps
- 2 onions
- 1 oz olives
- 1 tomato
- 1 zucchini
- 1 jalapeno
- 2 oz mozzarella cheese
- 2 oz cream
- 2 oz parmesan cheese (grated)
- 2 eggs
- 1 oz butter
- 2 cloves garlic (minced)
- 1 oz cornstarch
- 1 bunch cilantro
- 1 pinch cayenne pepper
- 1/4 teaspoons black pepper
- 1/4 teaspoons salt

xxxxxxxxxxxxxxxxxxxxxxxxxxxxxxxxxxxxxxxxxxxxx

How to Cook:

Thaw and peel the shrimp. Wash and cut the vegetables into small pieces.

Preheat the oven to a temperature of 350°F.

Sauté the onion until it becomes slightly brown. Grease a baking dish and put the onion in it. Then place layers of all the vegetables one above the other. Put the olives and shrimp in the uppermost layer.

Take a bowl and combine cornstarch, garlic, eggs, cream, and butter. Whisk them and make a smooth mixture.

Put this mixture on top of the vegetables and shrimp. Sprinkle black pepper, cayenne pepper, salt, mozzarella cheese, and grated parmesan cheese on top.

Bake for 40 minutes. Garnish with cilantro leaves before serving.

(39) Sweet Potatoes with Ginger

In this recipe, you are going to cook the sweet potatoes in butter. Curry leaves and ginger are an exquisite match for them. You can add honey or maple syrup towards the end to create an exotic bitter-sweet taste. It is not compulsory to cut the potatoes into small pieces. If you like, you can use them as big chunks. They will be equally tasty.

Total Prep Time: 30 minutes

Yield: 4

List of Ingredients:

- 1 lb. sweet potatoes
- 1/2 teaspoons ginger (grated)
- 5 sprigs curry leaves
- 1 teaspoon honey
- 2 oz butter
- 1/4 teaspoons salt

xxxxxxxxxxxxxxxxxxxxxxxxxxxxxxxxxxxxxxxxxxxxxxx

How to Cook:

Wash, peel, and cut the sweet potatoes into bite-sized pieces. Remove the curry leaves from the stem and wash them. Grate the ginger.

Melt the butter in a large pan. Add sweet potatoes, ginger, curry leaves, and salt.

Stir to mix everything properly.

Cover the pan and cook for 25 minutes.

Remove the lid. Add honey and cook for 5 minutes.

Transfer to a serving dish and serve.

(40) Salmon with Coconut and Cabbage

Here is a dish that has multiple health benefits. You will be using salmon that is an excellent source of Omega-3 fatty acids. It has a high content of potassium, iron, and vitamins. Cabbage is a bombshell of nutrients. It keeps a check on inflammation, improves heart health and digestion, lowers cholesterol levels, and has plenty of vitamin C and vitamin K. Coconut is rich in fiber. It is suitable for the heart, digestion, and weight loss. So, you can go ahead and pamper your taste buds with this fabulous recipe.

Total Prep Time: 20 minutes

Yield: 4

List of Ingredients:

- 1 lb. salmon fillets
- 1 lb. cabbage
- 2 oz shredded coconut
- 2 oz olive oil
- 1 oz avocado oil
- 1 onion
- 1 clove garlic
- 1/4 teaspoons coriander powder
- 1/8 teaspoons cayenne pepper
- 1/2 teaspoons turmeric
- 4 tablespoons fresh cilantro (chopped)
- 2 tablespoons fresh parsley (chopped)
- 1 lemon
- 1/2 cup butter
- 1 tablespoon peanut butter
- 1 oz olives (cut into halves)
- 1 oz acai berries
- 1/4 teaspoons black pepper
- 1/4 teaspoons salt

xxxxxxxxxxxxxxxxxxxxxxxxxxxxxxxxxxxxxxxxxxxxx

How to Cook:

Cut the fillets into 1" by 1" pieces.

Drizzle avocado oil on them.

Take a plate and combine shredded coconut, black pepper, salt, and turmeric. Toss the fillets in this mixture and coat them with coconut.

Heat olive oil in a pan and fry the fillet pieces until they become golden brown. Let them remain warm.

Chop the cabbage, onion, garlic, parsley, and cilantro finely.

Heat the butter in a pan and sauté garlic and onion. Cook until the onion becomes translucent.

Then add the cabbage, parsley, cilantro, lemon juice, coriander powder, cayenne pepper, remaining black pepper, and salt.

Cover the pan and cook for 10 minutes on medium heat. Stir frequently.

After that transfer, it to a large bowl and add the salmon pieces.

Garnish with olives, acai berries, and peanut butter before serving.

(41) Cabbage with Peas

It is a simple dish that you can prepare within 20 minutes. You can use any variety of cabbage for this recipe. But it is preferable to use white cabbage. Usually, the quantity decreases after cooking. So, do not worry if the pan looks too full in the beginning. It is better to boil the peas and then fry them with the cabbage to ensure that they get cooked properly. Lemon juice gives the dish a pleasant tangy touch. You can vary the amount of lemon according to your taste.

Total Prep Time: 20 minutes

Yield: 4

List of Ingredients:

- 1 large head of cabbage
- 4 oz peas
- 2 oz avocado oil
- 1 onion
- 1/4 teaspoons chili powder
- 1/2 teaspoons salt
- 1 lemon

xxxxxxxxxxxxxxxxxxxxxxxxxxxxxxxxxxxxxxxxxxxxx

How to Cook:

Grate the cabbage.

Cut the onion into small pieces.

Boil the peas for 10 minutes. Drain the water and keep it aside.

Take a large pan and heat the oil on medium heat.

Put the onions and cook for 5 minutes until they become translucent.

Then, put the cabbage, boiled peas, chili powder, and salt.

Stir to mix everything properly.

Cover the pan and cook for 10 minutes.

Then, remove the cover and cook for 5 minutes.

Cover it and allow it to cool slightly.

Transfer it to a serving dish. Squeeze a lemon on it before serving.

(42) Cod with Tomatoes

Maybe you are a busy mom and do not want to neglect your family's health. Here is a healthy recipe you can prepare in just 20 minutes. Your family will love the hot and sweet taste brought about by the mixture of sauces, vinegar, and lemon juice. By garnishing it with acai berries, you can add extra protein to the dish.

Total Prep Time: 20 minutes

Yield: 4

List of Ingredients:

- 24 oz cod fillets
- 2 oz olive oil
- 1/2 teaspoons chili sauce
- 1/2 teaspoons tomato sauce
- 1 teaspoon vinegar
- 1/2 teaspoons lime juice
- 4 oz tomato puree
- 2 cloves garlic
- 2 tomatoes
- 1 spring onion
- 2 bay leaves
- 1/4 teaspoons salt
- 1/4 teaspoons black pepper
- 1 sprig basil
- 1 sprig parsley
- 1/2 bunch cilantro
- 2 oz acai berries

xxxxxxxxxxxxxxxxxxxxxxxxxxxxxxxxxxxxxxxxxxx

How to Cook:

Chop the tomatoes, spring onion, basil, parsley, and cilantro. Heat one-ounce oil and sauté garlic, onion, and tomatoes. Add the tomato puree, chili sauce, tomato sauce, vinegar, lime juice, bay leaves, and a little salt and black pepper.

Cook for about 5 minutes. Stir well. Transfer the mixture to a bowl.

Season the cod fillets with pepper and salt. Pour 1-ounce oil into the pan. Put the fillets in the pan and cover it. Cook them on low heat for 5 minutes on each side until they become opaque and flake easily.

Then, pour the tomato mixture on the fillets and cook for another 5 minutes.

Garnish with basil, parsley, cilantro, and acai berries.

(43) Baked Carrots, Beetroot, and Peas

Here is a delicious dish for your family. The colorful vegetables make the recipe very attractive. As you know, carrots, beetroot, and peas are all very nutritious. You can enhance their value by cooking them with avocado oil and adding butter. Vinegar gives the dish a slightly tangy taste. If you like, you can use lemon juice instead of vinegar. You can even add some green vegetables to this recipe according to your preference.

Total Prep Time: 20 minutes

Yield: 4

List of Ingredients:

- 4 oz carrots
- 4 oz beetroot
- 4 oz peas
- 1/4 teaspoons ginger (grated)
- 1/4 teaspoons garlic powder
- 1 teaspoon onion powder
- 1 teaspoon vinegar
- 1/4 teaspoons salt
- 1 oz avocado oil
- 1 oz butter
- 2 tablespoons chives (finely chopped)

xxxxxxxxxxxxxxxxxxxxxxxxxxxxxxxxxxxxxxxxxxxxx

How to Cook:

Wash, peel, and cut the vegetables into small pieces. Grate the ginger.

Grease a baking dish and place the vegetables in it.

Sprinkle grated ginger, garlic powder, onion powder, salt, and vinegar on them.

Heat the oven to a temperature of 350°F.

Place the baking dish in it and bake for 15 minutes.

Take out the dish and add butter.

Bake for 5 minutes.

Garnish with finely chopped chives and serve.

(44) Cauliflower Rice

Maybe you are tired and bored of the staple varieties of rice and want to try something new. Cauliflower rice is a good substitute that can satisfy your urge for novelty in your culinary pursuits. It is not just nourishing but easy, too. All you have to do is use your food processor to grind the cauliflower florets into rice-like particles. Then cook it with eggs and stir fry vegetables just like fried rice.

Total Prep Time: 20 minutes

Yield: 2

List of Ingredients:

- 2 cups cauliflower florets
- 1 tablespoon sunflower oil
- 2 oz butter
- 2 cloves garlic
- 1 onion
- 2 spring onions
- 1/2 cup green beans (chopped)
- 2 oz olives (sliced)
- 1/2 cup carrots (chopped)
- 1/4 teaspoons salt
- 1/2 cup bell peppers (chopped)
- 2 eggs
- 1/2 cup potatoes (cut into pieces)
- 1 oz soy sauce
- 1/4 teaspoons black pepper
- 1 teaspoon chia seeds
- 1 oz cashew nuts
- 1 oz pistachios
- 1 tablespoon peanut butter
- 1 oz blueberries

xxxxxxxxxxxxxxxxxxxxxxxxxxxxxxxxxxxxxxxxxxxxx

How to Cook:

Put the cauliflower florets in the food processor. Pulse a few times so that the tiny pieces of cauliflower look like rice.

Whisk the eggs in a bowl. Heat oil in one pan and make scrambled eggs.

Chop the onion, spring onions, and garlic. Put one-ounce butter in another pan and sauté garlic, onion, and spring onions.

Then, stir fry all the vegetables. Transfer them to a bowl and keep them aside.

Put the remaining butter in the pan.

Cook cauliflower rice in it on medium heat. Stir occasionally.

Cook until it becomes golden brown.

Add the eggs, vegetables, olives, soy sauce, black pepper, salt, chia seeds, cashew nuts, and pistachios. Stir and mix all the items.

Cook for a few more minutes.

Garnish with peanut butter and blueberries. Serve warm.

(45) Multi-Layer Burgers

Your family will love this mouth-watering treat. It is an enchanting combination of meat, eggs, butter, mustard paste, mayonnaise, and tomato sauce. You can prepare the mayonnaise at home or buy it from the shop if you like. You can add some crunchy salad leaves to the buns and put a dollop of mayonnaise on top of each bun to make it look more attractive.

Total Prep Time: 15 minutes

Yield: 4

List of Ingredients:

- 8 oz meat (processed and ground)
- 2 eggs
- 2 oz olive oil
- 1 oz butter
- 1 oz mustard paste
- 2 oz mayonnaise
- 2 tablespoons tomato sauce
- 2 onions
- 2 tomatoes
- 1/2 teaspoons salt
- 1/2 teaspoons pepper
- 4 buns

xxxxxxxxxxxxxxxxxxxxxxxxxxxxxxxxxxxxxxxxxxxxx

How to Cook:

Put half of the oil in a pan and add the meat to it. Sprinkle half of the pepper and salt. Cook it until it becomes slightly brown.

Use the remaining oil, pepper, and salt to make scrambled eggs. Keep them aside.

Cut the tomatoes and onions into thin round slices. Cut the buns into halves.

Apply butter on the lower halves of the buns. Apply mayonnaise on the top halves.

Then, take the lower halves of the buns and apply the mustard paste.

Put a layer of onion slices on each bun.

Cut the scrambled eggs into halves. Place them on the onions.

Then, put a large spoon of browned meat on the scrambled eggs.

Place the tomato slices on top of the meat.

Pour tomato sauce generously on the buns and put their upper halves on top to complete the burger.

Press them slightly so that they remain intact.

(46) Honey Mustard Fillets

It is a hot and sweet recipe that combines the elegant taste of mustard with honey. The herbs add extra flavor to the dish. Your family will surely enjoy the fillets with their lovely taste and may even ask for more. You can use any variety of mustard paste and honey. If you like, you can use maple syrup instead of honey. It is not necessary to use dried herbs. You can use fresh herbs as well.

Total Prep Time: 20 minutes

Yield: 4

List of Ingredients:

- 8 cod fillets
- 2 oz mustard paste
- 2 oz honey
- 2 oz avocado oil
- 1/2 teaspoons garlic powder
- 1/2 teaspoons onion powder
- 1/2 teaspoons rosemary
- 1/2 teaspoons oregano
- 1/2 teaspoons thyme
- 1/2 teaspoons salt
- 1 sprig parsley (finely chopped)

xxxxxxxxxxxxxxxxxxxxxxxxxxxxxxxxxxxxxxxxxxxx

How to Cook:

Take a bowl and mix the honey, mustard, garlic powder, onion powder, rosemary, oregano, thyme, salt, and half of the oil.

Grease a baking tray with the remaining oil.

Apply a generous amount of honey-mustard paste on the fillets with a brush. And place them in the tray.

Heat the oven to a temperature of 350°F.

Bake for 20 minutes.

Take it out of the oven. Garnish with finely chopped fresh parsley and serve.

(47) Garlic Flavored Soya Chunk Skewers

Soak the soya chunks in hot water for half an hour. Then squeeze out the water and marinate them in a mixture of garlic and herbs. There is no need to cut the tomatoes and onions. See to it that they remain intact when you sauté them. Arrange the soya chunks with cherry tomatoes and small onions on the skewers. Then cook them on a grill for 20 minutes.

Total Prep Time: 20 minutes

Yield: 4

List of Ingredients:

- 1 lb. soya chunks
- 1/2 lb. small onions
- 1/2 lb. cherry tomatoes
- 2 oz avocado oil
- 1 teaspoon garlic powder
- 1/2 teaspoons oregano
- 1/2 teaspoons thyme
- 2 sprigs parsley
- 1 lemon
- 1/4 teaspoons chili powder
- 1/2 teaspoons salt
- 16 skewers

xxxxxxxxxxxxxxxxxxxxxxxxxxxxxxxxxxxxxxxxxxxxx

How to Cook:

Soak the soya chunks in hot water for half an hour before you start cooking.

Take a bowl and mix garlic powder, oregano, thyme, finely chopped parsley, chili powder, salt, and 1-ounce avocado oil. Squeeze the juice of 1 lemon. Whisk the mixture to combine the ingredients.

Squeeze out the water from the soya chunks and put them in the garlic mixture. Allow them to soak for 1 hour so that they are coated evenly with the mixture.

In the meantime, heat the remaining oil in a pan on medium heat. Sauté the onions for 5 minutes until they become slightly brown. Sprinkle a little salt. Remove them from the pan.

Sauté the tomatoes for 2 to 3 minutes. Sprinkle a little salt on them.

Take the soya chunks out of the garlic mixture and sauté them for 5 minutes.

Then arrange the soya chunks, whole cherry tomatoes, and small onions alternately on the skewers.

Heat the grill. Place the skewers on your grill. Cook them on each side for 2 to 3 minutes.

Keep them on a serving plate. Put the remaining garlic mixture on each of them with a spoon and serve.

(48) Novel Pizza Crust

You can surprise your family with this novel style of making a pizza crust. Unlike the regular pizza crusts, it is keto-friendly and gluten-free. You have to use cauliflower to make it. After softening cauliflower in the microwave, try to remove as much water as you can. It should be almost dry when you use it in the recipe. If you want the pizza to be spicy, use a chili or a hot and sweet sauce instead of tomato sauce.

Total Prep Time: 30 minutes

Yield: 4

List of Ingredients:

Crust:

- 2 large heads of cauliflower
- 1 egg
- 4 oz mozzarella cheese
- 1 oz avocado oil
- 1/2 teaspoons basil
- 1/2 teaspoons oregano
- 1/4 teaspoons salt

Topping:

- 4 tomatoes
- 2 onions
- 1 green bell pepper
- 1 red bell pepper
- 4 oz cream cheese
- 2 oz tomato sauce
- 1/4 teaspoons salt
- 1/4 teaspoons pepper
- 1 sprig parsley (finely chopped)

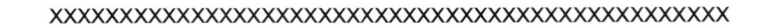

xxxxxxxxxxxxxxxxxxxxxxxxxxxxxxxxxxxxxxxxxxx

How to Cook:

Wash the vegetables.

Chop the tomatoes and onions into thin round slices.

Cut the bell peppers into small pieces.

Grate the mozzarella cheese. Whisk the egg in a bowl.

Cut the cauliflower into small florets. Then put it in your food processor and make cauliflower rice.

Place the ground cauliflower in a microwaveable container. Microwave it for 4 to 5 minutes. By then, it should become tender.

Then put it in a fine cloth and squeeze out the excess water.

Take a large bowl and mix cauliflower, egg, cheese, basil, oregano, and salt. Mix with your hands and make the dough for the crust.

Grease a baking sheet.

Divide the dough into four balls. Place the balls on the baking sheet and press them down to form flat circles. The diameter of each flat circle should be about 6".

Heat the oven to a temperature of 400°F.

Place the baking sheet in the oven and bake for 20 minutes. Then flip the crusts and bake for 5 minutes on the other side.

Remove from the oven and spread the cream cheese on each crust. Arrange the pepper pieces on it. Then put the tomato and onion slices.

Pour some tomato sauce on top.

Put the tray in the oven once again.

Bake for 5 minutes. Garnish with fresh parsley and serve.

(49) Butternut Squash with Lemon Ginger Sauce

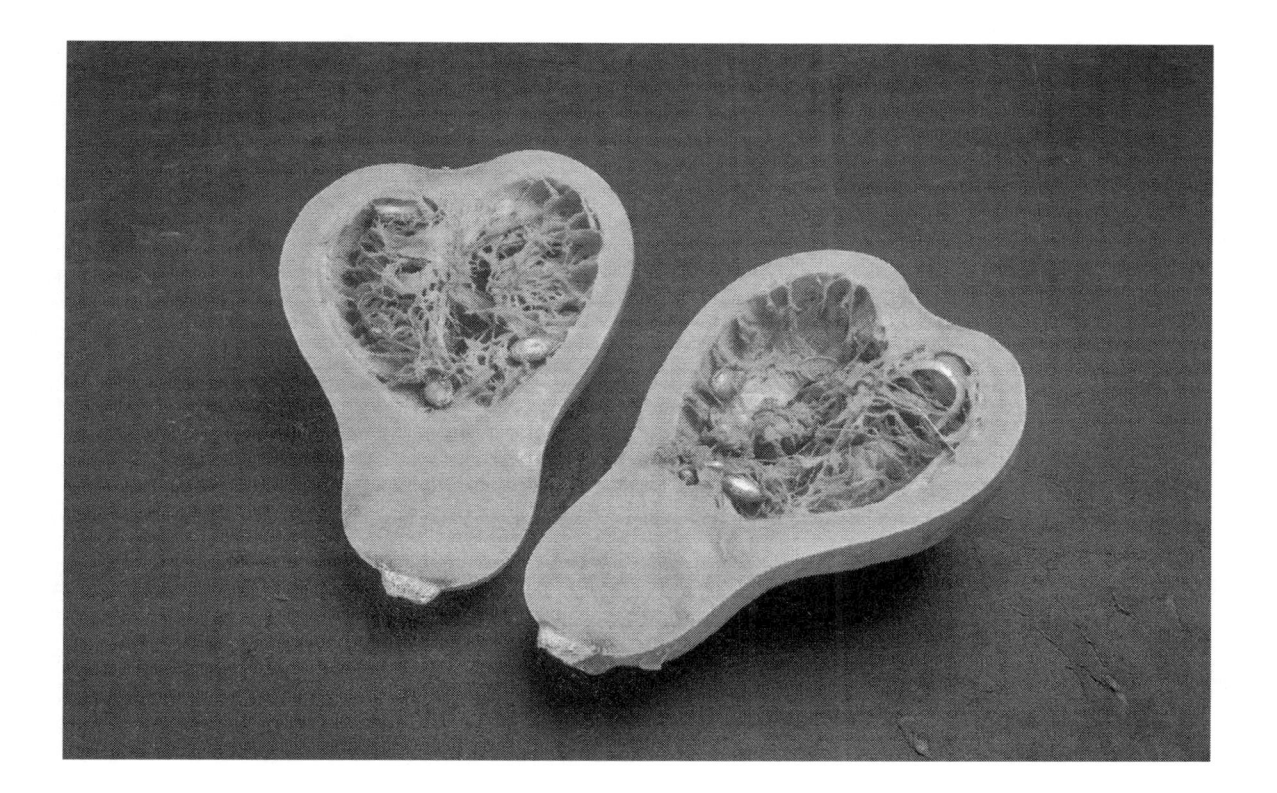

Here is a tangy dish that does not require too much preparation. You can prepare the lemon, ginger, and maple syrup mixture and add it to the butternut squash pieces. It is good to cut them into 1" cubes, but you can make the cubes smaller or bigger according to your preference. You can use more lemon or lemon zest to enhance the tangy flavor if you like.

Total Prep Time: 30 minutes

Yield: 4

List of Ingredients:

- 1 large butternut squash
- 2 tablespoons avocado oil
- 1 tablespoon lemon juice
- 1 tablespoon ginger (grated)
- 1 teaspoon maple syrup
- 1/2 teaspoons salt

xxxxxxxxxxxxxxxxxxxxxxxxxxxxxxxxxxxxxxxxxxxxx

How to Cook:

Peel the squash and cut it into 1" cubes.

Mix the lemon juice, ginger, maple syrup, and salt in a small bowl.

Grease a baking tray and put the butternut squash cubes in it. Coat with oil.

Pour the lemon juice mixture on them. Toss to coat the cubes evenly.

Heat the oven to a temperature of 350°F.

Place the baking tray in the oven when it is hot.

Roast for 20 minutes.

Then use a spatula to flip the cubes.

Cook for 10 minutes.

Transfer to a serving dish and serve.

(50) Delicious Tacos

Here is a dish loaded with flavorful items. These tacos will surely steal the show. You can use your favorite variety of meat for this dish. It contains parmesan cheese and heavy cream that makes it rich and tasty. Avocado fulfills many nutritional needs. And the exquisite combination of spices makes the dish delicious. Last but not least, it is a very filling and satisfying dish.

Total Prep Time: 20 minutes

Yield: 4

List of Ingredients:

- 1 lb. meat (processed and ground)
- 8 corn tortillas
- 4 oz peas
- 1 avocado
- 2 oz avocado oil
- 4 oz parmesan cheese
- 4 oz heavy cream
- 1/4 teaspoons ginger-garlic paste
- 1/4 teaspoons onion powder
- 1/4 teaspoons cumin powder
- 1/4 teaspoons pepper
- 1/2 teaspoons salt

xxxxxxxxxxxxxxxxxxxxxxxxxxxxxxxxxxxxxxxxxxxxx

How to Cook:

Peel and cut the avocado into small pieces. Grate the parmesan cheese.

Boil the peas for 10 minutes. Drain the water and keep them aside.

Heat half of the oil in a large pan.

Add the ginger-garlic paste and cook for 2 minutes.

Then add onion powder, cumin powder, pepper, and salt. Stir well and cook for 2 to 3 minutes.

Add the meat and peas to the pan. Stir to mix everything properly.

Cover the pan and cook for 15 minutes.

Remove the lid and add heavy cream.

Cook without covering for 5 minutes.

Allow the meat mixture to cool.

Grease a baking tray with the remaining oil.

Then spread the tortillas on it.

Put the meat mixture liberally on each tortilla.

Place a few pieces of avocado on top. Finally, sprinkle the grated parmesan cheese.

Roll up the tortillas.

Heat the oven to a temperature of 350°F.

Place the baking tray in it. Bake for 10 minutes until the cheese melts.

Transfer to a serving dish and serve.

About the Author

From a young age, Zoe loved being in the kitchen! More specifically, her uncle's bakery. Despite not actually working there, she would sit on the working table and watch herself get covered in flour over the next couple of hours. She also watched closely as her uncle kneaded the dough, measured out ingredients, and even decorated cakes. Even though she never tried doing it herself, she could recite the steps to most of the baked goods sold like her favorite song.

It wasn't until her 16th birthday, though, that she realized just how much she wanted to dedicate her life to making desserts too. No matter how much Zoe's mom insisted on buying a beautiful cake from a local bakery for her Sweet 16 party, Zoe wouldn't budge. She wanted to make the cake herself, and she did. Even though it wasn't the prettiest of cakes, it tasted delicious! Her whole family still remembers the flavor combo to this day: pistachio and orange cake. From there, things only got better!

After graduating from culinary school, Zoe worked in some of the finest bakeries throughout Europe. She wanted to learn from the best. Eventually, however, she decided to go back home and start her own business in Chicago, near her friends and family. That business is now one of the nicest bakeries in the city, which she has run with the help of her best friend, Lola, since 2015

Author's Afterthoughts

Hi there!

This is me trying to thank you for supporting my writing by purchasing my cookbook. I can't begin to express how much it means to me! Even though I've been doing this for quite a while now, I still love to know that people enjoy making my recipes, and I like to thank them for it personally.

You see, without you, my job would be meaningless. A cook with no one to eat their food? A cookbook author with no one to read their book? I need you to love my work to be rewarding, so do you?

One of the biggest ways to thank you for supporting me is by asking what you like or dislike most about my books. Are the recipes easy to follow? Do you think I should write more baking books, or what would you like to see more of? I will get to your suggestions for new books and improvements soon, ready to use them for my next book — so don't be shy!

THANK YOU.

ZOE MOORE

Made in the USA
Las Vegas, NV
10 October 2023